FOLK TALES OF THE WORLD
THE RABBI'S WISDOM

A Jewish Folk Tale from Eastern Europe

Retold by Erica Gordon
and Illustrated by Victor Ambrus

Bedrick/Blackie
New York

Snuggled in a valley somewhere in Poland was a little Jewish village. The people who lived in it worked hard from morning to night at sewing or blacksmithing, tinkering or farming. They were simple people, and if ever they came across anything at all complicated they went to their Rabbi to sort it out for them.

The Rabbi was a little man, as round as he was wise, with a long black coat tied with a girdle over his large stomach.

One day a man came to his door. He was terribly upset.

'Rabbi, Rabbi! Please help me!' he cried. 'My wife and I are very, very poor. We live in a tiny house, and we have eleven children, and my parents and my wife's parents all live with us. We are so crowded we have no room to move. And we're all so close to each other all the time that we get on each other's nerves.

Soon I will go mad! We will all go mad! Please Rabbi, tell me what to do!'

The Rabbi listened patiently. He kept silent for a long, long minute, scratching his head under his skull-cap and stroking his beard, to help him think. Finally he said to the poor man, 'What animals do you keep?'

'We have some chickens and ducks that give us eggs and we have a cow and a goat that give us milk,' he replied.

'Well,' said the Rabbi, 'if I am to advise you, you have to do exactly as I tell you, without asking any questions!'

'I promise!' said the poor man.

'When you get home, take all the animals out of your yard, and put them into your house, and keep them there all the time, day and night, night and day!'

Now it was the poor man's turn to scratch his head and think as he walked home through the higgledy-piggledy lanes. The stars shone and the moon was full, so he could see the cows in his neighbours' yards quietly settling down to sleep, and their chickens warmly nestled on their perches.

When he got home and was tucking into his nightly bowl of hot soup and black bread, he told his wife what the Rabbi had said.

'You've both taken leave of your senses!' she
shouted, waving a soup ladle at him.

But he had promised the Rabbi he would do exactly as he was told. So first he pushed all the chickens into the house, squawking and clucking. After them waddled the ducks, quacking snootily all the way! Then, very reluctantly, he led in the cow . . . and the goat . . .

After two days the poor man was back at the Rabbi's door, more miserable than ever.

'Rabbi, Rabbi!' he sobbed. 'You told me to put all the animals into my house, and I did as you said, and now things are even worse than before! It's just terrible! It's hot and it's smelly, and we all have to sleep so close together that the cow's nose was in my ear!'

'When you go home tonight,' said the Rabbi, 'let the chickens and the ducks out of the house and settle them back in the yard.'

So the poor man went home and did as he was told.
The next day he was back at the Rabbi's house
again.

'Well, Rabbi, I did as you said, and now there's no more quacking and squawking, and we no longer accidentally tread on any eggs laid on the floor. But it's still pretty terrible! The cow kicks everyone and makes an awful noise, and the goat, well, not wishing to offend you, Rabbi, it stinks . . .'

'This evening, when you go home, you must take the cow and put her back in her place in your yard,' replied the Rabbi.

The poor man went home to his long-suffering wife and the rest of his noisy, irritable family. They all stood watching as he led the reluctant cow out into the cold, wet night air.

The next day he was back at the Rabbi's house again.

'Life is a bit better now,' he said, 'but the goat still smells so awful and it keeps breaking everything and eating everything, and kicking everyone. It's driving us all mad!'

'Well, tonight when you go home, take the goat, and put it back out in the yard, with the chickens, the ducks and the cow.'

So the poor man went home and, with his whole family cheering him on, and the smallest child pushing from behind, he led the unhelpful goat back to its old home out in the yard.

Suddenly the little house became so quiet and peaceful! No more mooing or quacking, no more clucking or horrible smells! How wonderful it was!

The poor man was sure that none of his family would ever complain about anything ever again! As they all danced joyfully from empty room to empty room, he was sure they would live happily ever after.